Walter Smith

Lectures upon Drawing in the Three Grades of Primary,

Grammar and High Schools of the City of Boston

Walter Smith

Lectures upon Drawing in the Three Grades of Primary, Grammar and High Schools of the City of Boston

ISBN/EAN: 9783744776028

Printed in Europe, USA, Canada, Australia, Japan

Cover: Foto ©Paul-Georg Meister /pixelio.de

More available books at **www.hansebooks.com**

PAPERS PRINTED FOR THE USE OF STUDENTS IN THE MASSACHUSETTS STATE NORMAL ART SCHOOL.

LECTURES UPON DRAWING

IN THE

THREE GRADES OF PRIMARY, GRAMMAR, AND HIGH SCHOOLS OF THE CITY OF BOSTON.

ADDRESSED TO THE TEACHERS OF THE SEVERAL GRADES

BY

WALTER SMITH,

ART MASTER, LONDON, ENGLAND; DIRECTOR OF DRAWING IN BOSTON 1871 TO 1881;
PRINCIPAL OF THE NORMAL ART SCHOOL OF MASSACHUSETTS;
AND STATE DIRECTOR OF ART EDUCATION
IN MASSACHUSETTS.

BOSTON:

Rand, Avery, & Co., Printers to the Commonwealth,

117 FRANKLIN STREET.

1882.

To Past and Present Students of the Normal Art School.

———————

One copy of each printed paper issued from the school may be obtained by a past or present student of the school on application, in writing only, addressed to the Principal, WALTER SMITH. These papers should be kept by the students for reference.

Teachers of drawing in Massachusetts may also obtain one copy by making a similar application.

———————

DRAWING IN THE PRIMARY SCHOOLS.

[*Delivered, in 1881, in the Hall of the Girls' High School.*]

ADDRESSED TO TEACHERS OF PRIMARY SCHOOLS ONLY.

Mr. C. C. PERKINS, Chairman of meeting, briefly addressed the teachers.

MR. SMITH'S ADDRESS.

It is now ten years since the Industrial Drawing Act of this State of Massachusetts was passed by the Legislature, approved by the Governor, and became law.

By it the educational and industrial value of drawing was recognized. The place assigned to it was that of an element in general education on the plane of reading, writing, and arithmetic — not an optional but a required study, and to instruction in which every child in Massachusetts, whether to the manor born, or the stranger within her gates, has an inalienable right.

It is nearly ten years since the city of Boston, following her instincts of obedience to the law, and taking her claimed position as a leader in the van of educational progress, seriously set to work to accomplish what this law required.

What has been done, with this object in view, by city and by State, during the past ten years, is not altogether unimportant in the history of education here; but as both you and I have taken part in this period of educational development, and are therefore familiar with its features, though we can hardly be considered judges of its character, there is no need for dwelling at length upon details of the past.

But it may not be unprofitable to us, remembering the purpose for which we are assembled here to-day, if, after these ten years of our joint labors, I should briefly summarize some of the purposes we have kept in view, and the results of experience we have acquired.

As I am not privileged to address such a gathering of teachers as this very frequently in the city of Boston, and am fully aware of the valuable opportunity placed at my disposal now, I shall economize the time you give me by becoming brevity of introductory remarks, and devote myself chiefly to the task of making practical suggestions.

I see before me in this audience the faces of many who, nearly ten years ago, commenced with me, in those crowded and splendid classes in Appleton Street, the practical study of drawing, and of some who, since that time, have passed to their present positions through the Normal School, where they have been under my personal instruction. It is pleasant, after this relationship, to address you now as colleagues, and to bespeak your attention and patience for what I shall have to say on that ground.

You know that, though the teaching of industrial drawing in common schools was not a novelty in other countries, yet ten years ago it was regarded here as being in the nature of an experiment; and, besides having to encounter the serious deadweight of popular ignorance of the subject, its successful teaching involved the qualification of all the public-school teachers, young and old, by practice and study in a new subject, to give the instruction to pupils in the schools.

Great as was the diffidence many teachers felt and expressed in their ability to master the subject and to teach it, of their willingness to learn there was ample evidence by the attendance at the classes established for their instruction. The best proof of this is, that, out of one thousand and forty-five teachers employed last year in the public schools of Boston, only five had never attended normal instruction in drawing; and, out of one hundred and seventy-three schools, there were only three in which the teachers had passed no personal examination in drawing.

Such a record as that is creditable alike to the city which has provided the instruction, and to the teachers who have attended upon it.

Occasional exhibitions of class-work, produced under the instruction of the regular teachers, by the pupils of the schools, and their exercises at the annual or semi-annual examinations, show to demonstration that the personal study of drawing by the teachers has borne excellent fruits, and that, as a body, however various by comparison may be the attainments of individuals, the teachers of the public schools of Boston can teach drawing well.

I know that many of you do not think so, and this modesty is very becoming and delightful ; but you must pardon me for saying that you are not always the best judges of your own work in every department.

Probably every teacher here present has one or more pet subjects which she can teach splendidly, and, by comparison, thinks her teaching of drawing is a failure; and so, perhaps, of some other subjects. But that does not settle the question. There is, perhaps, a very natural and human danger that the subjects which are delightful to the teacher, and in which she has much skill, will be over-taught to the pupils; and that is as much to be regretted as that there should be any subjects in which the pupils are under-taught, through the absence of confidence in her own abilities, on the teacher's part. Yet I will assert further, that no teacher, to whose qualification to give instruction in the schools competent and impartial authorities have borne testimony, and who, on strength of that testimony, has tried to do the best she could for her pupils, whatever may be her own opinion about it, — no such teacher *has* failed of success in teaching, nor, as long as she loves her work and does her duty, can she ever fail.

I say this, not from any desire either to compliment or to comfort you, but because I honestly think that in this matter I am better able to judge than you are, from the stand-point of a specialist, and with the experience of a laborious lifetime wholly devoted to this subject.

There is another reason why teachers are sometimes suspicious of their own want of success in teaching drawing, when really there are no grounds for suspicion. The work to be done in drawing in the public schools, in order to be successfully and economically done, must be graded for the three grades of primary, grammar, and high schools ; and, in order to be progressive, no one of the three stages will tell the whole story, or be complete in itself.

Those engaged in teaching one of the stages are not always sure that their work is the best for that stage ; and unless they are familiar with the subject in all its stages, and see the relationship of one to the other, they are apt to consider their own work incomplete.

Yet it is not so necessarily. A teacher who would not be qualified to give instruction in drawing in high schools may be admirably qualified to do the work required in the primary schools, because the kind of work needed in one place is entirely out of place in the other.

To be able to judge the value of the work done and to be done in one grade of school, accurately and impartially, one must be familiar with and experienced in the subject and the processes of instruction in every grade of school, from the beginning to the end of school life; and that is something which no teacher, teaching only in one grade of the schools, and in but one class of that grade, can ever be expected to arrive at.

If it had not been my experience and occupation at different times to give instruction in all stages of the subject and in all grades of schools, from the lowest primary class to the graduating class of a normal art school, I should not presume to offer you an opinion on this matter, and ask you to accept it as practical and trustworthy. But having patiently gone through this experience as a teacher, and been employed to supervise and examine the work of other teachers in all these subjects and grades, I claim to be able to form a competent opinion upon the work now being done in the public schools of this city, in the subject of drawing, by the regular teachers of all grades of schools; and I ask you therefore to accept my opinion when I repeat that in every grade of school in this city the regular teachers are now eminently successful in teaching the subject of drawing. It seems to me to be my duty to state this much, and to do it very deliberately, before proceeding to the practical part of my address, both because you are entitled to it, and it will serve to explain why I have been asked to speak to you to-day. It is not because of any dissatisfaction with the work done in primary schools, nor for the purpose of suggesting any change in subjects or methods of instruction in them, but, on the contrary, to inform you that our progress is satisfactory, and to bring before your notice suggestions derived from observation of that progress, so that our advancement may be continuous, and our experience may be harvested.

I am to speak more especially on the course of instruction in the primary schools during the present half year. But as with one exception, and that the substitution of blank books for printed books in Classes 1 and 2, there is no change or alteration of work to be noticed, my suggestions will apply to the future as well as to the present. And as the work to be done in the third year, or Classes 1 and 2 of primary schools, is but a repetition on paper of what has already been done upon slates in the first and second year, or Classes 6, 5, 4, and 3, the same general observations will apply in all the classes.

Let us then see, first of all, what is the nature and object of industrial drawing in the public schools, and afterwards consider the part and stage of it which we have to provide for in primary schools.

Drawing, the ability first to see and then to express visibly the form, color, and character of created things, and, as a result of this ability, to devise and display original adaptations or arrangements which are the work of our imaginations, has an educational value apart from its industrial or commercial value.

It teaches us to see things, as distinct from looking at them, and gives us a language to express ourselves in, which is also capable of being made the test of true vision. The eye and the hand, the senses of sight and touch, are together equal to two-fifths of the soul's means of communication with the outer world. Their training and discipline, therefore, is not an unimportant part of that which we call education, — an exercise and stimulation of natural human faculties which require and await development in order to insure happy and profitable life.

It is because of the economic value in practical life of an observant and sensitive eye, and the usefulness to industry of that which is called a skilled hand, together with the great demand for skilled labor which now exists, and the creativeness and productiveness which that skill represents, that we have become accustomed to speak of the drawing we teach as *industrial* drawing, chiefly because of its pre-eminent value in the productive industries. But we might as well speak of the arithmetic we teach as industrial arithmetic, to guard ourselves from the suspicion of being engaged in the education of mathematicians; or describe instruction in writing as commercial penmanship, for fear the writing we teach may be used by an author or a statesman.

. Drawing is drawing, for whatever use it may be employed in the future; and it is because its educational use and practical value apply to all, that we justify it as a common element in practical education for our public schools.

It may help the mechanic to become a better workman, the professional man to devise or understand great constructive projects, and the general public to know and appreciate the true and the beautiful in nature and art.

But whether one, or neither, or all of these happen, is the concern of individuals; the work we have to do is to make it possible that all results may occur which can be expected to arise from a general diffusion of the common language of art.

Experience has proved that this alone can be done by systematically teaching the elements and grammar of this language in the same way and by the same means as we teach other branches of a common-school education, giving to each grade of school its own allotted work, and waiting patiently in this, as in all things, for the harvest which this seed-time may bring forth.

There is one phase of this work to be done in the primary schools, and that is by far the most important of all, for it affects all that follows it; another kind in the grammar and high schools, which develops the seed that has been planted; and lastly by practical life in the workshop, the office, or the world, which tests all this work as if by fire.

Our share of this work in the primary schools, then, is to prepare the pupils for their further and future practice in drawing by teaching them the alphabet and vocabulary of the language of form, and to accustom them to speak this language intelligently, whether by the tongue in form of words, or by the hand in shape of drawings, or by both name and shape uttered concurrently, as the most complete illustration of accurate knowledge, so far as ideas are concerned; and let it be never forgotten that ideas must precede skill.

To secure this concurrent use of word language and form language by the pupils, it would be profitable that at least one-fourth of the time devoted to drawing in primary schools should be spent by the pupils in drawing upon the blackboard answers to oral questions put by the teacher, the lips of the pupils being sometimes sealed. Thus the teacher asks, " What is a square?" and the answer, not a word being uttered, is a drawing on blackboard or slate by each pupil, of the form, or a family likeness of the form, of a square.

Reversing this process, suppose the teacher to become temporarily dumb, and the tongues of the pupils simultaneously untied. The teacher to draw on the blackboard a succession of simple forms, and the pupils' tasks to be the naming of them as fast as drawn.

This barter and interchange of the thought and the thing is education, productive of, though of infinitely greater importance than, what is called manual skill.

I earnestly commend to teachers the use of the blackboard and of drawing, to illustrate every subject they teach in primary schools, both by themselves and their pupils. Its value is altogether independent of artistic work, for blackboard illustrations can never be any thing but diagrams, and diagrams may teach principles, even when they are exaggerations, awakening thought and fixing ideas which are the very foundation of knowledge.

It has been said that " the blackboard is to *teaching* what steam is to transportation." Believing this to be true, and having witnessed its absolute truth in the matter of drawing, I would suggest that no lesson be ever given in this subject without full and generous use of the board by the teacher or the pupils, or by both.

In order to accomplish our work successfully, it is necessary to keep distinctly in view the objects we are striving for, and appreciate clearly the principles to be adhered to in securing them. Details of class management, or the adaptation of means to end, or the meeting of special difficulties and the individual failings of pupils, is the teacher's own work, with which no one should interfere, and about which little help can be given. But in the statement and consideration of general principles and objects to be secured, we may be of use to one another; and that is what seems to me to be now the most valuable use of our time.

Here, then, is a general statement of what should be expected from pupils in primary schools, in this matter of drawing; therefore, what the teachers should seek to develop and secure:

1. A knowledge of the alphabet and vocabulary of simple and regular form.

2. The power to draw such forms readily and with some precision, from the copy, from oral or verbal description, and from memory, and to be able to test the accuracy of their work by mechanical means.

3. To be able to analyze to some extent irregular forms, by comparison with the regular, and to draw the simpler examples.

4. To practise the arrangement of simple forms in new and orderly combinations.

Without at present going into details, it seems reasonable to expect so much from even little children, always supposing that they are made interested and happy in their work, that the standard of their attainments be not fixed too high, that information and thought be looked upon as the main things to be imparted and developed, and that manual skill be left to take care of itself.

I wish to make this statement about the unimportance of manual skill in little children as emphatic as possible, because so much mischief has arisen and harm done to education in drawing, by an over-estimate of its importance. Misled by this phantom which expects fifty-year-old skill in five-year-old bodies, and finding it not, teachers often misjudge their own excellent work, and think they have accomplished nothing. This is a serious educational mistake. The true test of success is the awakening of interest in the mind of the child about the forms and nature of the objects he sees around him, and the desire to express that interest by means of a drawing, if called upon to show what he knows about a certain object named. To secure this resort to illustration by the child, it must be practised by the teacher, and then comes in the value of the blackboard and drawing as an agent. It is not wise for a teacher to say that she is not skilled enough in drawing to illustrate on the board, for that is putting the cart before the horse. She should illustrate on the board *in order* to become skilled in drawing, if she is not so already. Do not refuse to go into the water until you know how to swim, but go there to learn.

In the schools of Quincy I have seen both teachers and pupils drawing on the board and on slates illustrations to stories and object-lessons, without apparently waiting to consider whether they could draw at all, or that drawing had any thing to do with the business in hand; which in one case was to show a wagon loaded with hay, drawn by four horses, the driver, whip in hand and holding the reins, being seated upon the load of hay. The boy who drew that was intensely interested and happy in his work. He was growing all the time; he was left to himself, and not worried by superior knowledge; and was learning, a good deal faster than text-books or teacher could have taught him, how to settle in his own mind, and display to the world, the problem of " What I know about a wagon and horses." Memory of his difficulties in making that picture was going to make him look at, and not only look at but see, a good many wagons as they passed him in the streets, or appeared in illustrated books or pictures; and that was a mental result and good education, which was not hindered by a certain look of antiquity about his wagon, or the strong family likeness among his four horses.

So let me urge that in addition to the work in drawing stated on the programme, and occasionally as a substitute for it, teachers should kindle a love and enthusiasm in their classes by giving the pupils full scope in a pictorial direction, and on favorite subjects to be chosen by the pupils themselves.

Let me remind you also, that we must no more expect uniformity of results from the instruction of a class of various pupils, than we should expect to find an agreement about politics or religion in a community of adults.

There is a good deal of difference between the size and thickness of skulls among children as well as among grown-up people, and as much difference between their antecedents and ancestors for a few hundreds of years. You cannot breed out of people in a year or two what it has taken twenty or thirty centuries to breed into them.

Slow children can be helped, but they do not need to be hurried; for it is often with them, as in mechanics, that what is lost in speed is gained in power, and that, if the speed be unnaturally increased in emulation of a lighter kind of machine, the tackling may give way, and both speed and power be destroyed.

We must not expect great improvement to occur very suddenly, nor is it a healthy sign; for gradual and rather slow growth, in which is assimilated the nourishment supplied, makes better and safer progress. You cannot extemporize either sound knowledge or cunning skill: there is no specific, nor recipe, nor royal road, nor short cut, by which you can abolish the influence of time on the maturing and healthy development of a human faculty.

Have patience with your pupils, and have patience with yourselves; for, as the beloved Physician said, "in your patience possess ye your souls."

You know that upon the programme there are to be given four exercises every week, and in the following order : —

1. Enlarging from card copies.
2. Reducing from copy on blackboard.
3. Drawing geometric definitions.

4. Dictation, memory, or design.

About each of these exercises I propose to make some suggestions, which I hope may be of some use to you, illustrated by the light of your own experience.

1. *Enlarging from Card Copies, and the Simplest Examples.* — Whether drawing upon slates or paper, it is intended that the pupils should make as large drawings as the limits of their spaces to draw upon will allow. Large drawings will always be much more improving than small ones, and take no longer time to make, whilst they are much more easily corrected.

Though a card may be placed in the hands of each pupil, thus furnishing the idea of what is going to be done, it does not give any information as to the order of the steps to be taken in doing the work. The whole exercise, therefore, from the first step to the last, should be drawn upon a large scale upon the blackboard by the teacher, as a guide, occasional reference only being made to the cards.

There are seventy examples on the first series, and fifty on the second series of cards; and each teacher should select from them only such subjects as her pupils can, without hurry, begin and finish in a lesson. For this reason, it is stated that only the simpler copies should be taken. Other examples will be found in the Manual, with which to vary the lessons, when the second exercise comes; viz., —

2. *Drawing from the Blackboard.* — Here also may be used such examples as the teacher may find useful, either from the cards or Manual, or of her own design, or selected from any other source. It is valuable to have the copy, about to be drawn, placed already on the board in its completed form, before commencing the lesson, so as to show very clearly to all what is going to be done. But, in drawing it before the pupils whilst the lesson is in progress, the class must be kept together as much as possible. To facilitate this, and to show the steps to be taken, it is useful also to have the diagram illustrated by three or four stages, beginning with the position and division of the first line. As that is done, upon slates or paper, the first stage to be erased from the board, and the second be begun; and so on until, the whole of the form being sketched, the work is to be completed from the finished example.

How much correction of the pupils' work is advisable? I am often asked. About that there is no hard and fast rule. It is well to correct one imperfection in the work of each pupil, if it should be apparent, but not more than one ; and very often it is well not to make any corrections at all on the exercise, but be content with directing the attention of the pupil to an obvious error, and say nothing about other imperfections. Thus recognize the principle that imperfect work is the consequence of imperfect thought, and, where you find that to be displayed, try to correct the imperfect thought in the child's mind, and the corrected thought will then dispose of the incorrect work. Never be troubled about always setting right with your own hand the untrue drawing on slate or paper, for that is only a symptom of the disease. Strike at the root of the disease in the thought-system, for thus only can it be cured. This of course cannot be done by one effort, either of teacher or pupil; but it makes a good deal of difference whether, by your method of teaching, the pupil is learning to draw, or only to make *drawings*, —just as, in learning a modern language, we want to learn to speak, rather than to make certain speeches.

Though I begin to despair of ever being understood on the question of where ruling and measuring and mechanical tests are permissible, and where objectionable, I shall continue to struggle with the subject.

There is a proper place and a right time for both mechanical and freehand work in drawing. Sometimes it is better that they should be quite distinct, and sometimes and on some subjects both may be employed in the same exercise. In the primary schools I would make this distinction. For the freehand work, in which there should be no ruling nor measuring, the first two exercises in each week, viz., drawing from the cards and blackboard, and drawing from the blackboard alone.

In drawing from dictation and memory, it may be left to the teacher's option whether all shall be done by freehand alone, or by ruling and measuring alone, when the subject is composed of straight lines; or partly ruled, as, for instance, the construction lines, and partly drawn by freehand, such as the curves.

In these exercises the whole class should work in one way, and the teacher decide which way, so as not to have some pupils ruling and measuring, and some drawing wholly by freehand.

The same option of the teacher may be extended to drawing of geometric definitions, and in the designing or arranging exercises all the mechanical means may be employed which are available, or that the pupils can use. It will simplify matters therefore, if we say that, for one-half of the work, viz., the first two exercises in each week, as stated on the programme, ruling and measuring are prohibited, and for the third and fourth, or all the rest, it is optional with the teacher how the work shall be done, with a recommendation towards variety.

The next exercise calling for some remark is, —

3. *Drawing Geometric Definitions.* — These exercises, which may be given either by the pupils copying blackboard illustrations, or from dictation, are of considerable importance, because they economize time in teaching and learning the other subjects, and are a definite contribution to that alphabet and vocabulary of the language of form, which I have described as being one of the principal objects of teaching drawing in the primary schools.

If these illustrations to the definitions be grouped together in the exercises, so that the distinct features of each may be made the more obvious by comparison with the rest, they may thus be taught quickly, and are not without interest.

Thus beginning with

LINES.

First Illustration. — A right line.
Second Illustration. — A right line vertical.
Third Illustration. — A right line horizontal.
Fourth Illustration. — Two lines parallel.

ANGLES.

First Example. — Any angle.
Second Example. — A right angle.
Third Example. — An obtuse angle.
Fourth Example. — An acute angle.

So with triangles, four-sided figures, polygons, and the circle ; and so on, with lines dividing figures, as diameters and diagonals, and thus explain, by drawing and having them drawn, all the terms and expressions and names which are made use of in teaching drawing.

These are not exercises to be dwelt upon for a long time, because of their interest, but should be practised as often as once a week, because of their use. They are specially adapted for the pupils to practise upon the blackboard with chalk, and on a large scale, either from dictation or memory.

If, after drawing rectangles, the pupils be allowed to convert them into houses, showing doors, windows, and chimneys, there will be some fun in the work. Or they might be allowed to follow Mons. Regamey's illustration of the geometric basis of art, by transforming any regular or irregular geometric shape into the likeness of any animal or natural form to which it is most like.

4. *Linear Designing — Memory and Dictation.* — The last exercise in each week is to be either in designing, memory drawing, or drawing from dictation, in sequence, every third week, so that one exercise of each kind shall come every three weeks.

Of the exercises in dictation and from memory, there is hardly need to say much, for teachers have had sufficient experience in both processes to know how much can be done by their pupils, how the subjects are to be handled, and what is to be sought for in either.

There is one feature of teaching a class to draw from dictation which seems to me valuable ; viz., that it enforces attention, and thus helps to form the habit. The words in which the exercise is dictated should be composed and written by the teacher, so as to be certain that the forms to be drawn are fully described in the clearest language, and in the fewest words, and, when the lesson is given, be read to the class. Fuller oral description should also be given in support of this ; but it is not wise to trust wholly to the suggestions of the moment for words or language of so great importance and consequence as those used in dictating a drawing lesson.

In primary schools, only examples containing straight lines and simple curves — or of compound curves, such as the ogee, made of two simple curves — should be given for dictation.

The work under the name designing would be more properly described as arranging, and I have already referred to it as "practising the arrangement of simple forms in new and orderly combinations," and also as "learning to arrange." Much of this must needs be done under the detailed direction of the teacher, who should decide upon both the form to be filled and the detail which is to be used in filling it.

Again : the enclosing form having been given, and divided into equal parts, it may be left entirely to the pupil to draw whatever may suggest itself to him in one division ; the only condition being that whatever is placed in one, shall be repeated as nearly as possible in all the others. It is a matter of little consequence what the unit of repetition is; for the real object of the exercise is to practise orderly arrangement more than to make an original design.

On a broad average, however, you will get rather more startling originality from an average class, than you know what to do with.

The kindergarten process of arranging colored sticks to form patterns is much the same as the designing to be followed in primary schools, — to give an outlet for ingenuity and love of change and the creativeness which we all have, but never so strongly as children have it.

Avoid giving much instruction about design. Let the children do as well or as badly as they like, and let them make their little attempts on slates first, even when they may have to draw their finished work on paper, so as to give them perfect freedom to experiment, to change their minds, to obliterate and begin over again, and wrestle with their subjects and with themselves.

I regard this exercise more as an amusement or recreation than any thing else; but it is a constructive one, and will help to counteract to some extent that other recreation, which comes better under the head of destructiveness or disarrangement, which children sometimes patronize.

In Classes 1 and 2 the work for the present half-year is to be in blank books instead of in printed books, in this matter reverting back to our practice previous to last year.

A clause in the recently issued plan of instruction modifies a paragraph in the directions printed on the cover of the blank-book. This paragraph says that the blank book of twenty pages is intended for forty exercises; but considering that there will necessarily be some time required for arranging the exercises on the pages, when guide lines and points are *not* given, it has been thought advisable to leave for each individual teacher's decision, whether one exercise or two shall be worked on each page of the books.

If only one exercise be drawn on a page, that will give an average of three lessons to each exercise, which will be ample time.

Let me recommend, also, that one-fourth of the time devoted to drawing, even in the first and second classes, should be spent at the blackboard by every pupil.

Also, that the diagrams drawn upon the board by the teachers for the freehand exercises should be on a large scale, with a central line of two feet six inches or a yard in length, so that all the pupils may see the example clearly.

You will find in the Manual, and upon the cards, a choice of examples for copies, with the exception o˙ dictation exercises; and these, it is considered, are best left to the skill of the teacher.

I have been asked by the Drawing Committee to suggest a course of examples upon the adopted programme, selected from the Manual, in order that those who may find it difficult to determine which examples are best may be assisted in their choice.

These have been drawn in a book, proportioned in size to the blank book, and occurring in regular sequence.

In this book, two exercises are drawn upon a page, for the convenience of those who may wish, or whose classes are able, to draw as many; but where, on the contrary, only one exercise is drawn, then I would recommend that the first half of this book be used to fill the blank book.

In conclusion, I now desire to remind you that we may reasonably expect to do as much for this subject in primary schools as is done for other subjects; that we ought not to try to do more, and should be content with no less.

In the opinion of competent judges, we are doing as much, though we are open to as much overhauling in this subject, as in others. There may be lacking some enthusiasm in our manner and methods of handling the subject; and I am prepared for such a criticism, for it has often been seriously objected, in the past, that we have thought too much about it as a subject of instruction, whilst it was yet a comparative novelty.

As this novelty wears off, let us hope that we shall gain in maturity what we lose in excitement, and that those who come after us may be benefited by our pioneer experience.

They may improve upon what we have done, and they ought to do so, to repay us for what we have done for them; but no future generation either of teachers or of the public, on this continent, can ever rob us of this historical achievement, that we have for the first time demonstrated to an unbelieving generation, that all human creatures are as much born artists, as that they are born to be inheritors of the kingdom of heaven. Education and religion are responsible for the rest.

DRAWING IN THE GRAMMAR SCHOOLS.

[*Delivered, in 1881, in the Girls' High School.*]

ADDRESSED TO TEACHERS OF GRAMMAR SCHOOLS ONLY.

———————

IT is pleasant, after nearly ten years of co-operation, to meet upon a plane on which there is no need to discuss the question whether it is possible that all children can learn to draw, or whether the regular teachers of the public schools can both learn and teach the subject. We have established the affirmative of those propositions long since, and in the teeth of a hostile and unbelieving generation ; which, however, has been so far not indifferent to our progress, that it has graciously humored us whilst we have been trying the experiment.

And, in consequence, we are here to-day to consider the next step in advance, which is, how best to teach the subject, conserving the progress made, and under circumstances which will test that progress.

It is also true that much has been done during the past decade to set people thinking about the practical value of drawing in education and in industry, and to attract the interested attention of sound and skilful educators in the subject ; yet it may with equal truth be said, that we have hardly yet touched the hem of the garment of this subject economically, whilst educationally our feet are scarcely upon the threshold of its temple.

Sternly practical people and nations are beginning to recognize the economic value in labor and life of an element not controlled by mere force, but controlling and directing it ; and are calling upon their educators to provide for and produce that element, and set it at work, much as the prophets of old called upon their gods for the divine fire that was to burn up the sacrifices upon their altars.

But you cannot extemporize experience — and that which we possess now has cost us ten years to acquire — without help or guidance from any external sources; so that although we have only made a beginning, trifling, perhaps, in comparison with the half-century's application of kindred people, and not yet so fruitful as the two centuries of effort made by the most artistic nation in the world, it is something to have begun seriously, and to have begun right.

Our progress has been somewhat hindered by the existence and healthy activity of sundry and manifold educational myths and delusions, from which other branches of learning have been delivered by the sanitary and winnowing and deodorizing operation of time. If we had done nothing more than to test common beliefs about drawing, to clear the track of obstructions made by ignorance, to prepare the way and make straight in the desert a highway for coming generations, then, and even then, the work done would be important and valuable, because of its initial character, for the first steps in a journey are of as much importance as the last.

I need not impress upon descendants of the Pilgrim Fathers, that the path of pioneers is always a hard road to travel, *for them*, whatever it may be for those who come after; and that is the path which you and I have been called upon to tread.

We are not at the end of it yet, though we may have made and set up certain landmarks, and milestones, and finger-posts on the road; and so it is well that we should, as now, occasionally meet together on a prospecting consultation for mutual encouragement, and to insure an economical division of the work to be done.

The subject which has brought us together on this occasion was communicated to me in the following words: —

Jan. 22, 1881, in Drawing Committee, —

"*Voted*, That the Director of Drawing be requested to address the primary and grammar school teachers on 'Authorized Methods of Instruction in Drawing,' and give them such counsel as they may require in the work of their respective grades."

That, then, is the object of our meeting to-day; and in order to confine myself to the subject, and to cover the ground as well, I have, as some of you know, asked by circular the principals of all the grammar schools in the city to suggest to me the questions they may wish to have answered, and the topics upon which they or their teachers may require counsel. I have to thank several masters for replies, and shall give to the questions they have propounded•the answers I am authorized to give by the Drawing Committee. This has seemed to me the most economical use of our time to-day, especially as our time is that of hundreds of persons; rather than that our meeting should resolve itself and degenerate into a discussion upon a few points, about which there ought to be great latitude of opinion among broad and healthy teachers.

If, therefore, I should omit reference to any special topic which you expected to hear about, you will at least give me credit for being anxious to know it from you beforehand, and thus to give it the benefit of deliberate consideration.

When I said just now that we were hardly yet on the threshold of this subject, the remark had reference more particularly to the whole subject of art education, as an element in professional, commercial, and industrial education and training; and not so much to that part of the whole subject which includes drawing in the public schools, which is, though of some importance to us, indeed but a very limited portion of the matter.

This undeveloped condition of a by no means insignificant department of human thought and activity — one so important, indeed, that it is capable of affecting national reputation and national prosperity (as it does to-day in the case of France and England) — is to be accounted for by the repelling influence of the mystery which has surrounded it in the past. This mystery, and the intellectual grasp which has been required to penetrate and dispel it, have made the subject somewhat unattractive to minds of the first order; or, if not wholly unattractive, there have been other fields so much more inviting and profitable, involving for their study and mastery a more circumscribed range of attainments and a more genial companionship in study, that the thinkers and workers in the general field of education have let this art department of it very much alone.

There is to-day no literature of art education; nor are there (with the exception of those in the department of architecture) any good text-books of the subject. Here and there a specialist has published his views about a detail or branch of practice, a mere thread of the whole woven fabric; but, up to the present time, no man or woman who can be faithfully described as thinker, artist, teacher, economist, has yet devoted the experience and maturity of a lifetime to the study and exposition of education in art. General education, letters, law, medicine, theology, trade, science, war, government, and even agriculture, have their literature and text-books; and each has leaders among men and women who are competent by professional knowledge and education, experience in detail, and practical acquaintance with the whole subject, to generalize sound principles from the varied experience of individuals and of nations. This is true in a limited degree also in the field of applied art, or of departments of it, like architecture or sculpture; but it is *not* true about *art education*, theoretical and practical, for economic, industrial, and artistic purposes.

By this absence of the highest form of matured authority — viz., a literature of the subject and leaders among men — we are placed at a great disadvantage, both in our study of it as a whole, and in our means of understanding the precise value and character of any department in it, in which we may be personally engaged.

For this reason we can consult no authorities, living or dead, and are left to pick our way, as best we can, from observations made as we go along, warned by failures and encouraged by what seems success, to be content to make our own precedents, and hew as near the line as we can plainly see it, dim and faint though it be. That is all we can do at present, until a mind of the first order — comprehensive, profound, and practical — having the student's habit, the teacher's instinct, and the economist's common-sense, shall come forward and lead us. May his advent be near, that we may be able to sing the *Nunc Dimittis* together, before we make our final exodus!

This slight introduction seemed to me to be necessary before we could modestly consider the first part of the subject, "*Authorized Methods of Instruction;*" for we must, in default of better, be our own authority, — judge, jury, plaintiff, defendant, counsel, and witnesses, all combined.

Let us then consider briefly what we have had to do, and how much we have already done in this matter, before we come to a reasonable conclusion about the nature and character of the work which we can best do, in the present and immediate future. And let us also not forget that we are considering the application to a subject of instruction, of the *general principles* of education, — not inventing specifics, nor debating various modes of teaching, but considering "authorized methods of instruction" in drawing, in this city of Boston, and to-day.

The Industrial Drawing Act of 1870 required that the subject should be taught in the public schools, and placed it among the elements of a general education; to instruction in which, every child attending the public schools had a right. It *might* have been grouped among the optional studies, or required to be taught in the high schools only. But, if you are interested enough in the matter to examine the chapter of the General Statutes, amended by the Act of 1870, you will see that the subjects of instruction among which drawing is grouped are reading, writing, and arithmetic, — not optional, but required; not for the benefit of a few, but for the education of all.

This involved two very important changes; viz., a change in the subject as then understood, and a change of teachers who taught it. The character of drawing, as taught in the schools up to that time, was such that it seemed only the gifted few could learn it, and only the teacher who had corresponding gifts could teach it. It was not, therefore, a general educational subject.

Here, however, we were confronted with a law which entirely ignored the whole theory of gifts, whether in teachers or the taught; and, to make the matter emphatic, it concluded with the gently insinuating words, "This act shall take effect on its passage." "Approved May 16, 1870."

The only persons who could carry out such a law were the regular teachers of the public schools; for at that time there were not special instructors enough in the whole country to teach the subject to all the children in the State of Massachusetts; and the only way in which the regular teachers could ever be expected to teach it was by simplifying the subject, so that it might easily be understood and practised by both all teachers and all children.

That was the task intrusted to our hands in 1871, just ten years ago, — and we have done it.

The principle underlying our plan was, that whatever it could be considered reasonable for the children to learn, it might be considered reasonable for the teachers to learn and to teach. The normal classes, which were at once commenced, were a recognition of this principle, and established its truth.

The chief corner-stone of our whole fabric was the use of the blackboard; and as the Superintendent had said, "The blackboard is to teaching, what steam is to transportation," we brought into use a very powerful instrument for our work.

You will most of you remember that the subjects studied during the first year, 1871–72, were freehand drawing of ornament from the board, showing only the two dimensions, length and breadth; model and object drawing, from the board and from the solid model, giving the three dimensions, length, breadth, and thickness; and memory and dictation drawing.

The next year, 1872–73, we took up geometrical drawing and perspective, both taught from the board; and in the following year, 1873–74, we introduced elementary design.

For several years afterwards, until, in fact, every teacher who intended to study the subjects had ample opportunities for doing so, these elementary classes were maintained; and last year I was enabled to report that, out of one thousand and forty-five teachers then employed in the public schools, one thousand and forty had attended normal lessons, either in the normal classes, the city normal school, or other normal schools.

The group of subjects which comprised this course of study, and for passing in which the second, or grammar grade, of teachers' certificate was awarded by the Drawing Committee, consisted of : —

1. Freehand drawing.
2. Model and object drawing.
3. Memory drawing.
4. Geometrical drawing.
5. Perspective drawing.

Afterwards, when design was taught, the memory-drawing examination became a drawing from memory of the teacher's own design, and has so remained.

Drawing from dictation is only a department of memory drawing, and not a distinct subject.

These five branches of drawing constitute, therefore, our solution of the question: "What kind, and how much, of drawing can be learned and taught by the teachers, and learned by the pupils in grammar schools ? "

You will remember that you were taught these subjects from the blackboard and in class, by means of class lessons given to all by the teacher, who made the diagram before your eyes, and explained its construction and character to you, whilst you were reproducing it.

That is how the mysterious subject of drawing was brought down from the clouds, where it had been regarded as the monopoly of genius and the prerogative of the gifted, and naturalized upon this earth in our class-rooms, the common property of all human creatures who possess the average intelligence.

It seems to me, then, that the most distinct feature of the instruction which you received, and have given to your own pupils, is the *method* in which it was given, and that method (which must not be confounded with the *subjects* of instruction) involves the use of the blackboard by the teacher in giving instruction; and its employment for that purpose at every lesson given by the teacher is most emphatically "*the* embodiment of the authorized method of giving instruction in drawing" in the public schools of the city of Boston.

About the *subjects* of instruction I shall have something to say further on; but here let me impress upon you, that if called upon to answer the question, "What is the authorized method of instruction in drawing in the Boston schools?" your reply would be, "The blackboard method, and class instruction." Just now we are required to rely more completely than before upon this authorized method of instruction; and I desire to point out to you that this is no reversal of principle, but a closer adhesion to it.

Whatever develops the self-reliance of the teacher, makes her more thoroughly the leader of the pupils; and no teacher so completely gains the confidence of her scholars, as she does when showing confidence in herself, by doing before their eyes, and step by step, the work she expects them to do for her.

Then, again, this method is the most economical of time in teaching a large number. It is impossible to give private lessons in public schools; for the time devoted to one subject, such as drawing, is insufficient for more than the teaching of principles to the whole class, which every individual in it should be made to understand.

This is so completely proved to be true, that, even in the high schools and free evening drawing schools, both of them one grade higher than grammar schools, the use of flat copies by the pupils is confined to the reproduction of those made by the teacher, before and for the whole class, and no flat copies of any kind are allowed in the hands of the pupils. This is being done when the subjects are light and shade from the cast, or studies in color from objects, which are, you will allow, more difficult and elaborate than any thing taught hitherto wholly by class instruction, or than can ever be expected in grammar schools.

Understand me, I am not objecting to text-books; for I believe in them when they are of the right sort — which, unhappily, is not always the case; and, when of the wrong sort, we are infinitely better without them.

And there is a better thing than even a good text-book, and that is a good teacher.

But we do want some good text-books in the hands of our good teachers; and especially now is there need of analytical and exhaustive manuals on the subjects of perspective, model-drawing, and design, for the use of teachers.

I had hoped to have been permitted, through the kindness and forbearance of my admiring friends, to have assisted you who are my colleagues, and the cause of education generally, by preparing such works myself.

The French have a proverb that "it is the *impossible* which always happens;" and who knows but this apparent impossibility may actually occur?

If I should not be allowed so to help you, perhaps the hint from me that such manuals are wanted will be sufficient, and untold and indescribable varieties of them will be immediately produced.

Let us now consider the *subjects* of the instruction in drawing in the grammar schools, and endeavor to see what should be the aim of the teacher in giving the instruction.

We must not forget that the prime object sought for in requiring drawing to be taught in the schools was the development and elevation of industrial skill and public taste. This must to a great degree determine the character and nature of the work to be done, and control the processes to some extent by which we do the work.

It must be definitely practical, such as is required by practical people who make use of drawing for any useful purpose, whether in the workshop for constructive purposes, or in the designing-room for the expression of taste and originality.

Thus it must include the elements of scientific drawing: its language, to give knowledge of the vocabulary of form ; and its modes of securing accurate results, to insure that all which depends on exactness shall be available and understood.

It must develop the taste by familiarizing the pupils' eyes and hands with accepted types of the beautiful in art and in nature ; and it must exercise and cultivate the originating faculty, the creativeness which is essentially human, — for we are told that man alone is a designing animal, — thereby to give opportunity to apply and combine the two elements of science and art, constructiveness and taste, which the two branches of instrumental and freehand practice have taught us the language of.

For this reason we include geometrical drawing with instruments, to secure all that is valuable and necessary in true and accurate workmanship ; freehand drawing of ornament and objects, to obtain a knowledge of appearances and beautiful forms unattainable by mechanical means; and elementary designing, to develop the imagination, and learn the processes of applying drawing to practical and industrial purposes. Just how much of all these objects can be secured in each grade of our public schools, depends upon ourselves as teachers. If we are content to do our share in each grade, without expecting to do all; and if we work on sound educational principles, aiming to get as much as possible out of each of these branches of drawing for the information and cultivation of the minds of our pupils, as well as the exercise of their hands, — then we shall teach the subject as sensibly, as profitably, and as fruitfully as it can be taught.

But we cannot do every thing in any one of the three grades, though the bulk of the work will be in the central or grammar grade. On the lower side of this centre will be the work of preparation, done in the primary schools; and on the farther side the work of application, carried out in the high schools.

Between these two, and the heart of both, comes what I will call the work of education in the grammar schools.

Before going into detail, and being fully aware of the healthy variation of attainments both of teachers and pupils in the grammar schools, and the necessary and unnecessary imperfections in our work, I yet, with perhaps as long, as broad, and as thorough a knowledge of this subject of drawing, both here and elsewhere, as is required to form an accurate judgment, make bold to say, and take the full responsibility of saying, and all which that implies, that the subject of drawing has been, and is, better, more sensibly, and more successfully taught in the grammar schools of Boston, than in any other grade of schools in any city in the whole world.

It requires some knowlege of drawing in the public schools of all countries and civilized nations of the world, and some experience, to decide what *is* good work, from a stand-point which takes in the whole field of art education, to be able to make such a statement. And let me remind you of the important factor, that it requires at least an equal amount of experience and knowledge to be competent to contradict it; for less qualified persons, though they may mean well, do not know enough to give an opinion that is worth any thing on this particular subject.

It is only the just due of the teachers in the higher classes of grammar schools, that their work should be thus acknowledged; for it has long since been my opinion that it deserves the character described in the statement I have made.

Contradiction is now in order, if it can be made by competent people ; and if it BE made by any one who can be so described, between now and the next time I am privileged to address you, it shall be considered by me, and the grounds of it conveyed to you.

I hope you will allow me to say that in this matter I am imitating the example of the shoemaker who stuck to his last; for this judgment comes within the legitimate range of my professional business as a teacher. And out of respect for the teacher's profession I will add, that it is because I know it requires as much devotion of life and labor and brains as any other profession, and practical experience in it is of as much value as in any other, that I have said what I have about *competent* judges, and will not acknowledge the competence to be judges of those who take up this business as an amusement, late in life, and become critics of our work, because they have nothing else to do.

Fellow-teachers, it is because I have taught this subject of drawing in every grade of school represented in the public schools of this city, and in every class of those schools, from the entering class of the primary school to the graduating class of the professional art and science school, and every subject in all those grades, — that, on behalf of the teacher's profession, I assert for it the same authority and privileges of knowledge and experiences which are readily accorded to all other professions, and are their just due. And because of this experience I have presumed with some degree of confidence to express this professional opinion to you about your work, and to do it with the widest publicity, because I know it to be profoundly true, and ask you to accept it until a more competent and more authorized judgment be forthcoming.

Speaking now of the subjects of instruction in drawing in the grammar schools, and commencing with the three upper classes, 1, 2, and 3, it will be seen, by reference to the printed plan of instruction, that the same subjects are to be studied in each class, and the same number of pages in the blank books to be devoted to each subject. The subjects and proportion of the twenty pages of the book given to each are as follows: freehand, six pages; model and object, six pages; geometrical, six pages; design, two pages.

I may as well here take this opportunity to answer two questions put to me by some of the masters. The first is, whether, in freehand, object-drawing, and design, one or two exercises are to be drawn on a page? In reply to this, I quote from the printed programme: "Whether one or two exercises are to be drawn on each page, is to be determined by the teacher, according to the circumstances of the class and progress of the pupils." The same applies to the freehand, model, dictation, and memory exercises of the three lower classes, 4, 5, and 6. The second question is one which, like a wandering, guilty spirit, refuses to be laid at rest, either by church, state, or education. It is, "In what subjects are ruling and measuring and mechanical aids permitted, and where objectionable? May straight lines be ruled in model-drawing?"

As I have said before, our drawing, to be useful, must be practical, and must include the scientific and mechanical, as well as the artistic and tasteful. Both elements are indispensable, and each possesses features unattainable in the other. Neither alone tells the whole story of practical drawing, and therefore neither should be alone practised to the exclusion of the other. But it is judicious in teaching to reserve some exercises wholly for one kind of practice, some wholly for another kind, and in some to make use of both resources — instrumental and freehand — in the same exercise.

The four branches of practice for Classes 1, 2, and 3, as they appear upon the printed programme, are, first, freehand ; second, model-drawing.   Upon these two branches I would have no ruling nor measuring, nor guide points nor tracing paper, ever permitted under any circumstances.   Upon the next two — third, geometrical ; fourth, design — all the mechanical helps possible should be employed, and the proper use of them thus be taught to all pupils.   The programme itself, on p. 2, states that in the subjects of memory and dictation drawing, in the Classes 4, 5, 6, it is optional with the teacher whether the exercises shall be performed with the assistance of mechanical means or without that help.

Let me, then, finally, recapitulate what is to be considered the rule in our schools about mechanical help.

In freehand and model drawing it is *forbidden.*

In geometrical and design it is *required.*

In all other exercises it is *optional.*

I will now proceed to make some suggestions on these subjects in the order in which they stand upon the programme : —

1. *Freehand Drawing.* — The work in the blank books is to be a review of that which has already been done in the books, — not necessarily a repetition of the same exercises, but of similar ones, the teacher drawing the example on the board for the class to copy.   A certain number of pages of the Freehand Manual, from which to select copies, are suggested for each class ; but this need not be strictly adhered to, if the teacher prefers to select others.   You have the whole Manual to select from, and can therefore adapt your selections to the capabilities of your several classes.   The examples should be drawn upon the board upon a large scale — say two feet six inches, or a yard in height — in its complete form, before the lesson begins ; and, whilst it is being given, should be repeated by the teacher, step by step, before the class.   When the finished example is drawn previously, the diagram made by the teacher whilst the class is drawing need not be so exact or elaborate as it would require to be, were no finished diagram available for reference.

To vary the practice, one or more copies might be drawn upon the board by the teacher, to be drawn by the class without such detailed instructions as have been described ; or one-half of a symmetrical example, or one unit in a rosette, be given, and the pupils be required to draw the rest without a copy.

Allow me to suggest that in all freehand, model-drawing, or designing exercises, a section of the class, say one-fourth, be put to draw upon a large scale on the blackboard. This bold practice will greatly improve the freedom of hand and sense of proportion of the pupils, and also make the drawing upon paper more rapid and accurate. Serious mistakes, which would be passed over, or not be seen, upon a small scale on paper, will become intolerable when perpetrated upon a large scale on the board. This may somewhat interfere with keeping the class together in their work in the books; but that could be remedied by giving two lessons to each exercise, and letting a fourth of the class spend one-half of the time of each lesson at the board, and three-fourths of the class at the same time to be drawing in the books.

Thus, in a class of forty pupils having two lessons of forty-five minutes on one exercise, or ninety minutes in all, the pupils Nos. 1 to 10 to draw on the board the first half of the first lesson, and Nos. 11 to 40 to draw in their books. During the second half of the first lesson, Nos. 11 to 20 to continue the work on the board, begun by the first ten, and all the rest of the class to draw in the books; the third and fourth sections of ten in each to do the same upon the second lesson, and thus complete the exercise.

2. *Model and Object Drawing.* — I have been asked "whether it is a waste of time to draw the copy, for practice, on slates before drawing it in the book." That partly depends upon how well the class can draw; but in model-drawing it seems to me it would be a saving of time, and even in other subjects it could not be a waste of time. But it might occupy more time than the class could afford to give.

Whether the object-drawing be from the solid model, or from blackboard, the pupils should draw the subject first from the board; and it then might be convenient to let this explanatory and trial exercise be drawn on slates, or on the board, which would be better.

The class-rooms are so arranged that it is impossible to teach object-drawing from the solid satisfactorily. The principles of drawing regular geometric forms can, however, be taught from the board, and be illustrated by the solid model and the object if placed in as good a position as can be found on the teacher's desk.

There ought to be one room in every grammar school, with the seats and desks ranged round it, in a circle or hollow square, leaving a broad open space in the centre for the model or object to be placed, so that occasionally an object could be seen below the level of the eye.   Or, if it would not be considered sacrilege, a corner of the hall might be used temporarily a few times in the year, to secure a good view of a model for the upper classes, — one class at a time.

Those of us who have taught classes to draw from the solid know what an amazing fertility the average pupil develops in drawing that which it is impossible to see with the human eye, and in refusing to see the true shape of the object to be placed before him.

It is impossible to account for it.   Among all the thousands of persons I have seen commence the practice of drawing from objects, whether young or old, not one has ever apparently seen an object, even approximately, as it appears to the eye, and, with a persistency worthy of a better cause, insists upon drawing it wrongly.   There is no cure for this but practice, but it suggests how much reliance you can place upon the statement any one makes about the form of any thing, unless he can draw it.   I would not believe the evidence under oath, about the shape or appearance of any created thing, given by the saintliest person in the world, if his impressions resulted from his own eyesight as a witness, *unless he could draw*.   Appearances and facts are not the same once in a thousand times; and unless he can deduce the appearances from the facts, and the facts from the appearances, he is not to be believed about the facts.

I regard this subject of object-drawing from solids as being one, which, under the present arrangement of the class-rooms, must be difficult to teach ; and suggest that the fullest explanations and complete illustrations by diagrams be given by the teacher at every lesson.   It is better to teach the principles of perspective as applied to objects, well, than to have objects drawn from by the class, which cannot be seen, or seen only in distorted views or unusual positions.   By this I mean, that to put a chair, for instance, which is usually seen below the eye, to stand upon the teacher's desk as a model, so that it will be seen above the eye, and the under surface of the seat seen for the first time in the lives of the pupils, is to make a hard subject of drawing harder still.   It would be better to have the geometric solids in such positions; for they are not associated with any particular places in our minds, and are as likely to be seen above as below the eye, and in one place as in another. The subjects suggested in the programme are such as it is supposed can be obtained in every grammar school.

3. *Geometrical Drawing.* — About the problems in geometrical drawing I would suggest that they be worked upon as large a scale as possible to get the required number done upon the allotted number of pages. Not more than six and not less than two problems should appear on each page. And among them the geometric shapes selected for the designs should here be first worked out.

The best result to be shown from this branch of study ought to appear in the drawing of these regular forms, both enclosing and forming part of the exercises in design, for that is applying a knowledge of geometrical drawing to practical and workmanlike purposes. And that is also where the usefulness and influence of the study best shows itself.

When, three years ago, I submitted a set of memory exercises in design, the work of the graduating classes of two of our grammar schools, to a distinguished inspector of art schools in England, he was struck with two features in the work: one was the amount done in the time, and the other was the originality of the designs. But he was simply *amazed* at the accuracy and workmanship of the geometrical drawing in the enclosing forms, and in the spacing out of the surface to be covered.

It is through this use of instruments, to secure exact work when accuracy is essential, that drawing becomes of practical use to industry; and, among all the branches of it, none is so completely industrial in its character, and useful in its applications, as geometrical drawing.

4. *Design.* — Some years ago, when design was a novelty in our schools, and had become somewhat a favorite study, an impression was created among the teachers that elaboration of arrangement and multiplicity of detail constituted excellence. The illustrations of elementary design, drawn upon a very small scale in the Manual, were partly responsible for this impression, which, nevertheless, was a great mistake. If any one of the designs in the Manual were to be enlarged so as to fill a whole page, or even half a page, of one of the drawing-books, the arrangement would then appear simple, and by no means crowded with detail.

But a change, which is also an improvement, has been observable during the last two or three years. A greater simplicity of treatment, with details on a larger scale, has prevailed.

Yet I judge, from the examination exercises and occasional exhibitions, that, in the higher classes, there is still room for improvement in this direction.

Nevertheless, if called upon to furnish some examples of drawing, by which the method and the work done in the Boston schools could be best judged, I should not hesitate at once to select the drawings from memory of the pupils' own designs, made by the graduating classes of the grammar schools, at their diploma examinations. They are simply wonderful, and have been so pronounced by very competent judges.

I would, however, suggest that, in the lower classes, a pleasing arrangement of very few leaves, or leaves and flowers, treated in a simple manner, should be sought for in preference to great originality, or profusion and elaboration of material.

I have recently defined elementary designing as being, " to practise the arrangement of simple forms in new and orderly combinations ; " and this I commend to your attention.

DICTATION DRAWING.

The value of drawing from oral direction cannot be over-estimated, either in its practical influence upon teaching drawing, and the ease which results from it, or in its indirect bearing upon other studies. It develops habits of attention and thought, and teaches the value and importance of words. By it the teacher can show how necessary it is to begin a drawing with its most characteristic feature, as, for instance, by the central vertical line or axis of a symmetrical design ; and also to determine the chief proportions before attending to details or subdivisions. It fosters the habit of working deliberately, without hurry, and enforces the value of doing one thing at a time, and doing it well. It shows the teacher also how much of form can be expressed in words, and what must depend upon the observation and taste of the pupil. It is a simple way of exercising and developing the imagination about the real and concrete ; and, of all the branches of drawing practised, it is the most profitable in teaching the alphabet, the vocabulary, and nomenclature of simple, regular, and exact form.

Commencing with the illustrations to geometrical definitions, and proceeding by reviews and memory exercises to fix them in the mind and memory, the teacher may establish between the class and herself, by means of dictation drawing, such a realizing and appreciation of the significance of language, that every word uttered, either alone or in connection with others, will be canvassed mentally, and its meaning interpreted.

It seems to me that the fostering of such a habit in a mild and gentle way, and by an exercise which is partly physical, and never about abstract ideas, is a healthy educational process. In order to be sure that you may do all that will be expected of you in the several classes, I give you this practical counsel — to all : —

Let every teacher take one of the blank books, and space it out into the number of pages required to be given to each branch in her particular class, according to the programme. And here I will answer another of the questions put to me, viz., "Are the different kinds of exercises to be drawn together, or alternated in the book?" The answer is, Whichever the teacher thinks best; but it is convenient to have the exercises together. Thus, for the Classes 1, 2, and 3, the pages 1 to 6, freehand; 7 to 12, object; 13 to 18, geometrical; 19 and 20, design. In the Classes 4, 5, 6, it would be better to alternate the exercises, in order the better to maintain the interest of the younger children. To resume the story of the teacher's blank book.

Having paged off the book into subjects, I would then make selection of every exercise in each subject which it seemed to me the class could best do; and, as a guide for myself, I would sketch out every freehand exercise, and place it just where, upon the page, I should want the scholars to draw it, and the size it should be drawn, to fill the page agreeably. And repeat this process with the other subjects.

Thus, having planned the course according to the strength or weakness of the class, you will be able to direct and lead the work without loss of time, and have all the strength which comes from not only preparing every lesson beforehand, but from having fixed its place in your half-year's work as well.

With the programme, "The Freehand Manual," and a copy of the work done from September to February before you, it will be a comparatively simple matter to make such an arrangement. The sketches need only be rough suggestions, for I know you have not time to do more, but doing that much will not only save your own time and that of your pupils, but add greatly to the confidence with which you will teach all the subjects in the class-room.

I used to notice, when one-half of the drawing-books consisted of blank sheets, the best work was always to be found on those blank pages, wherever the teacher was interested in the subject. The opportunity we now have will enable you to show the best work all through the book.

Let all the diagrams and exercises be as large as possible, and well and truly centred and placed on the page. There is as much judgment and workmanlike habit developed by the practice given in adapting the example to the page, as in balancing the opposite sides of a symmetrical object; and it is an introduction to the valuable mental and moral process of cutting your coat according to your cloth.

This spacing and centring of the paper is valuable practice, as every draughtsman knows who has ever made a working drawing; and it should therefore not be dispensed with in the teaching of industrial drawing.

GENERAL SUGGESTIONS.

It is believed, and in my opinion justly, that to give the grammar-school teachers of this city a blank book for their pupils, and ask them to review in it what has been done before by their classes, is, for a temporary exercise at any rate, safe and profitable.

They are not asked to extemporize pictures as copies, but simply to teach very elementary truths to their pupils, always remembering that the most valuable result to be obtained by the scholar, and therefore sought after by the teacher, is a mental one, not alone a picture of the truth in the pupil's drawing-book, but the truth itself in the pupil's mind.

I know that the teachers are able to do this work, and it is nothing new; but I could not have said so much a few years ago. There has, however, been a considerable advance in the feeling of confidence and self-reliance within the past three years on the part of the teachers, which encourages the Drawing Committee to believe that printed copy-books may be safely dispensed with for a time.

It is, of course, to be expected that the best teachers will not be satisfied with their own performances in teaching drawing and it is extremely modest and beautiful in them to be otherwise than self-satisfied.

Good authorities, however, have expressed a high opinion of our work in drawing in the grammar schools, and you have been told what I think.

There is sometimes, among teachers, a disinclination to draw freely on the blackboard for purposes of illustration in teaching other subjects, and to provide copies when teaching drawing.

Let me ask you all to realize that the only way to become ready and expressive upon the board, and with chalk, is to steadily draw every thing you want to illustrate a lesson by, whether of drawing or any other subject. You cannot learn to swim unless you go into the water, and you cannot draw well upon the board unless you draw upon it *somehow, until* you draw well. The French have a proverb, " They forge well who *forge ;* " and it applies also to blackboard drawing.

Then, it is well that teachers should remember that in these exercises in drawing, they are not exercising artistic acrobats, but educating children, and by such exercises, and not training them to produce drawings; for the drawings in their books are of no more value, in view of the result sought, than are the numerals in the sums in arithmetic, which have been worked upon and have vanished from their slates.

The thing we have to do for children is to teach them to think, and to think rightly, to develop the ability to analyze and compare ; to distinguish between the right and the wrong, between the beautiful and that which is not beautiful, between the true and the false ; and to incline them to choose the right, and the beautiful, and the true, by their own mental action.

That is education ; and whether the means by which we give the knowledge of facts, or excite the emotions to produce the mental act of choice, be arithmetic or drawing, the result to be looked for is the same ; and the process and manual exercise through which it is done are only the means, never the end, and relatively therefore of little importance.

I am led to impress this upon you because teachers sometimes show me the books of their scholars, and apologize for imperfect work in them. There is no need for such apologies : if the work is honest, it *must* be imperfect, and, if the teacher is faithful and fair to all alike, it *must* be very varied in attainment. Uniformity in the manipulative processes, the outward and visible signs of instruction, in any class-room, means cruelty to animals, and there is no other way of accounting for it; and that is something which is simply detestable.

What we are trying to do in our lessons is, to make the children know *how* to draw, not how to make drawings; and I hope you see the distinction. And the great reason for teaching them to draw is, that the process of drawing makes ignorance visible: it is a criticism made by ourselves on our own perceptions, and gives physical evidence that we either think rightly or wrongly, or even do not think at all.

For a bad or incorrect drawing is never an accident: it is an uncomfortably accurate mirror of our thoughts, and fixes the stage of mental development and civilization we have arrived at.

Good or bad pictures are never produced unintentionally: they have existed in the brain in all their beauty or deformity before they passed through the nerves and fingers on to the paper or canvas. So with drawings: if a child draws in a diabolical manner, don't trouble so much to alter the drawing in his book, as to change the mental process in his skull. That is where the mischief springs from, and it is the only place where it can be cured.

In conclusion, I think it is rather an advantage than otherwise, that, by circumstances over which we have apparently no control, and by authority which it is our duty to recognize and respect, we should, as teachers, be thrown upon our own resources to review a subject that we all know. It is a precedent not unlikely to be followed in the interests of true education, that the work of the first half of the school year should be reviewed and made more thorough in the second half, by being gone over a second time, instead of our undertaking other work, new and fresh.

This change, made now for the first time, will involve no new departure from the method of instruction hitherto pursued, nor the introduction of any new subject, nor the imposition of work not done before at some period of our experience, in the maturing and development of this subject of instruction in public schools.

For ten years we have worked together; not only for drawing, and in the city of Boston, but for the organization and establishment of a neglected though important element in education, for the use and benefit of all who live on this continent.

Recently a distinguished expert in educational matters, representative of the most artistic nation upon this earth, said of Boston, that it was the only city in the world where all the children were taught to draw well by the regular teachers. If we have cause for satisfaction in this, it is because education has thereby been advanced in a natural and legitimate direction, from which it will never retreat so long as our mother-tongue is spoken in this land.

And this has been accomplished, not by systems, nor text-books, nor specialists like myself, but by the faithfulness of the regular teachers, and by the educational instincts of the race to which we all belong. That is *something* which the labors of our youth, the devotion of our lives, and the character of our common ancestors have given to us, and which nothing can ever take away from us while we live, move, and have our being. And upon that *something*, fellow-teachers, we must all now depend.

DRAWING IN THE HIGH SCHOOLS.

[*Delivered, in 1879, in the Normal School.*]

ADDRESSED TO TEACHERS OF THE HIGH SCHOOLS ONLY.

———

In the year 1870 the Drawing Committee of the School Board of the city of Boston issued a report in print, in which occurs this sentence : —

" Of all the studies in our public schools, drawing exhibits the most feeble results. We have had no system. Our teachers have not been instructed, and the work must now be commenced. Shall we have a plan ? or shall all be done at random? "

In the year 1876 another report was printed, not this time by the Drawing Committee of Boston, but by the French Commissioners on Education sent to the Centennial Exhibition at Philadelphia. They had there subjected the exhibit in drawing made by this city to the closest scrutiny, and presented to the French Government a very analytical and exhaustive report upon the whole subject of industrial drawing as displayed in the exhibition. After finding some slight faults with the materials used in our treatment of the subject, and noticing the comparative exhibit of all the States, they say, —

" The public schools of Massachusetts presented a collective exhibit extremely remarkable, the most complete of all, and the most methodically arranged."

Again, —

" Such as these works are, they bear witness to the excellence of the method, to the good disposition of the scholars, as well as the conscientious and intelligent care given to the instruction with the view of developing the practice of practical elementary drawing. If we bear in mind that these fruits are the result of two years of trial, we must admit that never before have such remarkable results in so short a time been attained."

In drawing inferences from their study of the whole subject and contemplation of the works displayed, the Commissioners make this suggestion : —

"It is necessary that France defend her pre-eminence in art, hitherto uncontested. With us, as elsewhere, it does not suffice to have excellent special teachers of drawing : *it is necessary that all the teachers should be able to give the first instruction in drawing in the day classes to the entire school population.*"

I put these two statements of two very different bodies of men before you for the purpose of asking whether the question of the Drawing Committee of 1870, when they asked, "Shall we have a plan?" has not been answered by our experience and testified to by competent authorities.

And when they promised — after making the statement, "Our teachers have not been instructed" — that "the work must now be commenced," I would ask, Has not the Drawing Committee kept its promise? The work has certainly commenced, and the teachers have been instructed; and we are here to-day because it is not yet completed.

If France acknowledges that we are preparing to contest her pre-eminence in art, and suggests to her government the adoption of our plan as her defence, — viz., the employment of all the regular teachers of the public schools to teach the subject, and give the first instruction, — it appears to me that we certainly have a plan, and that all is not now "done at random," as it was in 1870.

Fellow-teachers, the most earnest and conscientious amongst us are often distracted in our work by the squeaking of penny trumpets of disapprobation; so let us not ignore this diapason of recognition from the most artistic nation in the whole world.

Were I a clergyman, and about to preach a sermon, I should take, as a text, "Great is thy faith: be it unto thee even as thou wilt."

Eight years ago I stood on this platform, and enunciated the doctrine that adult teachers might learn to draw and become proficient teachers of drawing to their pupils, if they would only try to do so, on the one condition that they should have faith in themselves, and be as patient with themselves in trying to learn as they would be with their pupils when teaching them other subjects. This belief of mine was not very generally acquiesced in; but a large proportion of the teachers, a vast majority of all the Boston teachers now in the city's employment and in all the grades of schools, were willing to try to learn drawing and to teach it, and have tried diligently and faithfully. And it was the result of this trial, as evidenced in the works of their scholars, which drew from the French *savants* the words of commendation I have quoted; and they were deserved.

This occurred to me as a fitting introduction to what I have to say to-day, because we are now on the threshold of another new departure in this matter, as characteristic, and involving as much faith on your part to insure its success, as that original change made eight years ago.

You all know that the School Committee has decided to withdraw the special teachers of drawing from the high schools after the close of the present school year, principally as a matter of economy; the initiative in this step having been taken by the Committee on Revision, not by the Drawing Committee. Next year, then, the regular teachers of the high schools will be required to give the instruction in drawing to their pupils in the same way as the primary and grammar school teachers already have done for several years to their pupils; for it has been assumed that the high-school teachers are at least as capable as those of any other grade.

The remarkable success of teachers in the higher grammar classes has made it necessary, if progress is to be maintained, that some subjects of instruction in the high schools should be developed and improved; and, in the general revision of studies made for the schools, the subject of drawing has been re-arranged, to bring it into true educational sequence with that which precedes it, and into harmony with the improved possibilities, as well as the needs, of the present day.

The revised plan which has been adopted by the School Committee contemplates the carrying-out of the new order, commencing in September, 1880; and it is to prepare the teachers for this work that the Drawing Committee has provided this special class for high-school teachers. The suggestion is also made, that, so long as special teachers are employed, the regular teachers of the high schools should work out the exercises done by their pupils in class under the special teachers during the current year; also that additional practice may be obtained by attending one of the free evening drawing classes, of which there are six in the city. And this last suggestion is not made with the view of monopolizing the spare time of the teachers, but only to point out that plenty of opportunities exist for obtaining instruction by those who desire it, or who do not feel qualified to hold their positions in the high schools to the satisfaction of the School Committee without such instruction.

We have to carry on this subject now into one grade higher than the second or grammar grade, and it will be to attain this third grade for the high-school teachers that the principal efforts of the Drawing Committee and myself will be directed this year.

Before entering into details concerning the revised course of study, I desire to make some general observations upon teaching this subject, and commend them to your consideration as teachers.

We have no need in this quarter of the nineteenth century, or in any intelligent community, to ask whether all children can be taught to draw, or whether all teachers can teach the subject in the public schools of all grades. These are settled issues in all progressive countries, and in all but very drowsy communities. What concerns us now is *how* it can be taught so as to secure the best practical results educationally and industrially; and just at present the question we have to consider is, How can high-school teachers qualify themselves, if not already fitted, to do this work for their pupils?

I must here appeal to both your faith and patience, — the faith which can remove mountains, and the patience in which we are told we can alone possess our souls. You begin this additional year's study well prepared by previous study and practice on the second or grammar grade; and, though it cannot be supposed that you will teach the subject to your pupils at the end of your first year of study as well as you will after several years of practice in teaching, yet in making this beginning you have only to attack a difficulty which has been already overcome by the grammar-school teachers, and you begin it with infinitely better preparation.

You will need to attend this class once a week for two hours, and will require some time for home practice, to work out the lessons here given; for, as you well know, work done by yourself has a certain kind of influence not like that done in the class-room. And you must never forget that you will only have to teach drawing as an element in general education, not as an art or specialty.

How, and to what extent, should drawing be taught in high schools ?

Let us first recognize that to justify its place in the public schools it must be made educational to all, not only to a few ; and this properly limits the range of instruction to general education, and prohibits its treatment as a special subject, requiring professional skill of a special character in the teachers.   Drawing has the same relation to art that language has to literature.   As a specialty, as picture-making, for the accomplishment of the few, or the recreation of the few, it ought to have no place in public schools supported by the taxes of all.

But if it develops observation in all, opens the eyes of many to the beauties of nature and art, leads the few to discover unsuspected powers in themselves, fits many to become skilful in industry and all to become a refined constituency for the development of great national capacities and industries, utilizing mental and physical resources of the people and the country, — then it may well be supported by the public, and taught to all in the public schools, as something which is of general advantage.

To adapt the subject so as to comply with this condition, it was necessary to abolish the mere picture-making as taught by the old generation of drawing-masters to the few pupils who were supposed to have talent, — a method which was as unphilosophical in theory as it was unsuccessful in practice, leading only to sorrow and travail in the pupils, and the delusion or disgust of parents.   Whatever may be the character of the exercises made by pupils, the only results of any value arising from teaching drawing in the public schools are to be found in the minds of the pupil, not on their drawing-paper.   If all the drawings ever made in public schools were to be collected into one heap, and made into a bonfire, and the destruction decreased by a feather's weight the results of the education given, then the instruction has been misdirected.   The subjects taught, and text-books or examples used, are only opportunities for giving or obtaining useful information, or to develop, by practice, a certain amount of that which is sometimes wrongly called *manual* skill, on the same plane as the mental perception.   I purposely say " wrongly called ;" for manual skill, as distinct from intellectual perception, or as being in a different stage of development from it, does not exist.

Each lesson or exercise in drawing, or any other branch of education, is merely the peg upon which a teacher can hang a certain amount of information, or by which he can irritate into action the mental powers of his pupils; and the work of the pupil is the record of what has taken place, the first step toward assimilating the information, or displaying the inventive powers which have been aroused or called into play. The value or efficiency of the lesson is not therefore to be measured only by the beauty of the drawing made by a pupil, but by the evidence it gives of having made him think new thoughts and cast away old ignorance, seen with a keener vision, or comprehended a revealed beauty. It is consistent with good instruction, therefore, that the manual work of pupils may be very unskilful, whilst the teaching may have been excellent, and the educational process be manifest. If the drawings display an effort to express some grammatical truth of form, or illustrate a principle in graphic representation, however clumsily expressed, the teaching has been good; but, if all the drawings show the same mistakes in an important principle, the pupils must have been badly taught. [As a practical teacher, I would, however, like to make one exception to this general statement: I have never seen or heard of a pupil, who, however good the teaching, did not at the beginning of his practice make retreating parallel lines to diverge, instead of making them converge, as they really appear to do.] Notwithstanding individual deficiencies in the taste or handiness of pupils, it is easy enough to see if a truth has been comprehended, even if there be an artistic stammering in its utterance, which is a matter of temporary habit only. In my opinion one of the least valuable results of teaching drawing in the public schools is, that the pupils will learn to draw; for thousands will be benefited by the education it gives, for one who will be helped by practising the art in his future vocation.

In my own practice, as the Principal of two Normal Art Schools, I have observed that those who are studying to become teachers of drawing display their possession or deficiency of the true teacher's instinct by the manner in which they practise teaching as a normal exercise. Some will go round to the pupils who are engaged each on a separate work, look at the

drawing, sit down, and carefully correct its errors on the drawing itself with their own hands, saying little or nothing to
the pupil, passing on to the next, and repeating the same process of instruction, so called; as though the teacher's business
was to pick people out of the mire, instead of teaching them
to walk so that they would not fall into it.   Those are the
aspirants who will never become teachers (though they may fill
the positions and draw the salaries), unless they can be made
to see their radical error of method, and change their system
of instruction.

Others there are, who, from their first efforts at teaching,
display instinctively the habit of creating an improving desire
in the pupil, and regard a wrong or faulty drawing as evidence
of something misunderstood in the pupil's mind, or as the result
of insufficient or confused thinking.   Instead of setting to
work and altering the symptoms of the disease which show
themselves on the paper, they go behind the symptoms, and
attack the disease itself in the mind of the pupil, eradicating
the cause, and letting the effect take care of itself.   Those are,
in my opinion, the students who will become teachers.

It is better to correct the thought which produces the wrong
drawing, than to correct the wrong drawing which is the product
of the wrong thought; though it may sometimes be necessary
to operate on the drawing, not to beautify, but to destroy it,
if need be, in order to demonstrate the erroneous thinking.

I suppose this to be true in other subjects as well as in
drawing.   If a teacher of arithmetic found in a sum worked
by a pupil the numeral 3 where a 5 ought to be, he would
hardly go to work to show the scholar how to patch up the 3,
and put a head on it so as to convert it into a 5; but would
point out the false step in the calculation, so that the scholar
seeing his error would become dissatisfied with his 3, and be
impatient to score his 5.

That is precisely how I would correct a drawing; in the
thought of a pupil, and make him correct it upon his paper as
evidence of his improved knowledge.

I have often tried to impress upon the many teachers who
have attended my lessons in this building, that drawing may
be said to have two elements, — the first relating to matters of
fact, the scientific element; and the second relating to matters
of feeling, dependent on taste.   It is a great comfort to know

that a large proportion of educational drawing, the elements
we have to teach, belong to the domain of fact, about which
there is no more mystery, nor can it be more a subject of con-
troversy than is a proposition in Euclid, — no more and no less.
No amount of sentiment or difference of opinion can change a
scientific law, though it is easy enough for people to be wholly
ignorant of it, or misunderstand it in the degree of their
ignorance. We reach solid ground when we get to the representation of regular forms in defined positions by means of
perspective or model drawing; and the effects of light and
shade upon regular or irregular objects depend upon the operation of laws which are as old as the sun, and as unchangeable.
The true form and appearance of a definable object under
given conditions, whether as to its size, outline, or effect of
light and shade upon it when in one light, are all as definite
and demonstrable, and the representation of them as much a
matter of right and wrong, as any other scientific facts in the
world of physics. That is incontrovertible.

People may argue in a circle to all eternity about a certain
painter's eye for color, or the appreciation which another artist
has for aërial perspective, and become as unanimous about it as
they are about religion and politics; but neither sentiment nor
culture changes the law of form or of light and shadow, any
more than they can affect the truth of the multiplication-table,
or change the law of gravitation.

There is a scientific element in all drawing and in all art,
which must be regarded if the drawing is to be true. There is
a right and a wrong about the delineation of form and light
and shade, which can be learned by all who are intelligent
enough to learn any thing, — a law that will never wear out or
go out of fashion; and it is a comfort to know that the appreciation of this prime element in all intelligent art is a matter
of the understanding, which all teachers are supposed to possess, and not one of that indefinable attribute called taste,
which does not seem to be so common, and which some people,
even teachers, are often willing to say they are deficient of.
Clearness of understanding will therefore be the chief qualification to become a possible teacher of drawing upon the basis
on which we shall have to teach it.

There are other features in drawing, such as the use of color,
an eye for proportion, harmony, and contrast in design, which

do depend upon taste for their excellence. But even in these departments a higher law prevails, and harmony of color is as much a question of law as harmony in music; so also there are true principles of design based on a study of nature's laws, and the practice of the best schools and masters, which are very definite in application, and incontrovertible. The teacher should, however, as a rule, not vex himself or his pupils about these features into which the element of individual taste enters, and is so important, but adhere to sound grammatical principles and processes in the elements of drawing. We are all of us more or less color-blind, and no man ever yet was catholic enough to love the art of the Greek and the Goth with equal affection.

The differences and even the idiosyncrasies of good taste are to be respected; for this variety in choice and preference is a great charm in all things. Some people are narrow enough to believe that there is only one right and one wrong in all matters, whether of fact or of opinion; and yet we find that, except in the main lines of creation, nature is perpetually varying her productions, seeming to contradict herself out of the very wantonness of profusion, as if she was afraid we should form too low an estimate of her wealth and playfulness, — laughing to scorn our picayune observations, and deriding us from a higher plane than that we stand upon, one which includes the small and few things we have perceived, in a vast horizon which stretches beyond our narrow vision.

It is a remarkable fact that the great men of the world seem to have become great in spite of their education, and often in precisely those departments of thought or action in which they were never instructed except by nature and observation. So it would appear that all we can really do for a healthy child is to educate his faculties, and leave the rest to nature and time; above all things to avoid teaching tricks or specifics, or the idea that any process or knowledge is complete or final, and that in the work of education there is only so much to learn, and then we must be satisfied.

I think it necessary to say so much to you, because in your departments of instruction so many things are fixed and unchangeable, — as, for instance, grammar and geography and arithmetic; and you might therefore interpret what I have said about the facts of drawing as limiting the scope of your teaching in the subject to the mere physical laws of appearance, ignoring the higher developments of poetical renderings of nature, or the wealth of a fertile imagination, which has often detected the true type in many varieties, and can formulate the very highest generalization.

Let us believe in the infinite capacity of all our pupils, though we cannot distinguish the great from the small whilst they are in our care. Give them all credit for being the raw material of great men, and teach them all we know of the eternal principles, leaving to them the responsibility of doing what they can with the truths, the modest truths, we have been able to impress upon them.

We must give all our pupils credit for having the faculties of each, and remember that a faculty, like a limb, may become stunted and withered if its existence be ignored, or it be never exercised. It is this recognition of its existence, no matter in how crude or limited a form, and the judicious appeal to and exercise of it, that develops and makes it healthy. I would repeat that we are too apt to believe or assume without thinking, that the child's education is confined to or measured by the time spent in the schoolroom, forgetting that every thing, from the air we breathe to the very sleep we take, is either educating or destroying us. The child surrounded in its home life by an atmosphere of taste and culture will be naturally more sensitive to ideas and forms of the beautiful than one who is not so happily circumstanced : but that is not a difference in faculty, but rather one of readiness to assimilate instruction easily; and even in this matter the race is not always to the swift.

There is one feature in teaching applied design to your pupils which I ought to point out to you, and it illustrates that which I have just said. It is no more intended or expected that all who design shall become designers, than that all who make Latin verses shall become poets. The exercise is disciplinary of common faculties, not of special abilities. Pupils are thereby taught to exercise their creative and originating instincts, to arrange and express their thoughts in the language of form, to secure a defined result, just as they are instructed in the use of their mother tongue or any verbal language by the exercise of writing original compositions in it. It is much to be hoped that all who practise English composition will not become authors, though they may be educated and made more useful citizens by writing good English. So it is with designing. It is to develop observation and originality, and create a habit of method and order and love of accuracy in their work, that pupils are taught to design ; to give them scope to display the best and the worst that is in them ; and to substitute the best for the worst under careful 'guidance, and for the development of their constructive and creative faculties. It will also directly exercise the imagination, and necessitate habits of observation ; for nothing so opens the eyes of people to the art work which is often to be seen surrounding them as the task of having to create something of the same kind imposed upon themselves. Then for the first time many begin to see what others have done when such a task was given to them, and know what it is to plan and arrange and test the value of the actual knowledge they have acquired.

You must not expect very good designs from your pupils, remembering how very seldom you get good work from even professional designers. Not one design in six made by the latter is carried out into execution, and not one in ten is fit to be. So remember to be merciful in criticising the designs made by high-school boys and girls, regarding them only as testimony of their thinking, the symptoms of their mental affections, which you have to make a diagnosis of, and prescribe for, for each individually as the symptoms vary.

The remarkable success and ingenuity displayed in the graduating classes of grammar schools lead us to hope that each year will give us pupils for the high schools better prepared than before in this as well as in every other branch of drawing.

In teaching perspective and model drawing, though it is necessary to teach by illustration and repetition certain fundamental principles of representation, certain definitions and axioms, yet the mere word-repetition, or being, as the actors say, word-perfect, in them, will not necessarily shed light upon their work in practice. Yet I am not averse to requiring the pupil to repeat a rule he knows and has often complied with, if he, and whenever he, deliberately outrages it in his practice through indolence or want of attention ; and calling upon him in the light of his better knowledge, to correct his own bad work by help of an awakened memory or conscience. But this appeal to formula is open to abuse. Some of the teachers in primary schools make a mistake in that direction about the geometric definitions when teaching them to young children; and, as a similar mistake may be made about the axioms of perspective and model drawing, I will here repeat to you a statement lately prepared for them about the mode of teaching definitions: —

"It is to be understood that the learning by drawing the diagrams of geometrical definitions is intended to give children correct ideas of the position of lines and the character of regular and to some extent of irregular forms. This is not to be confounded with *memorizing* the words of the definition, which may be done in a mechanical way without grasping the idea of the form described, and thus be useless and monotonous labor. The correct idea of a line or form (as for instance of an oblique line or an equilateral triangle) should come first, then the drawing of the form which expresses it, and lastly the words which define it. If the child possesses the true idea of a form, and proves its understanding by drawing the illustration as accurately as a child may be expected to do it without cruelty in the teaching, the definition has been learned, and the most accurate and concise way of defining the form in words will afterwards be easily learned, because those words will represent and express knowledge already in the child's mind. But the words without the ideas represent nothing to the child, and therefore the committal of them to memory should be waited for, and not expected or insisted upon, at first. The theory of a definition in words is, that it should reflect an image which already exists in the child's mind, and not be a substitute for that image, uttered by the tongue."

I should apologize to you for speaking about *memorizing;* for I confess to being unable to comprehend the meaning of the word as sometimes used by teachers. There are some things which were never committed to memory in the sense which some people seem to attach to that expression, but which can never be forgotten whilst life and reason remain; and there are others which can never be remembered, whatever trick be resorted to to keep them in mind. I expect most people can remember what they understand, if it is of sufficient importance to them to remember, and this applies especially to principles; and they forget that which they cannot understand, or which they believe to be of little consequence. What boy ever tried to memorize the place in the orchard where that particular tree grew upon which the first ripe apples appeared at summer-time? And yet where was there ever a boy, who, once knowing it, ever forgot the place?

Drawing from memory is merely testing the knowledge you have retained of that which you have once learned; but the manner in which you have learned it, and extent to which you have known it, will determine your remembrance of the fact, and no formal memorizing will keep you in that.

I propose now to refer in detail to subjects which form a part of the revised course for high schools, and with which we shall have to struggle in this class for instruction in the third grade.

CLASS INSTRUCTION FROM THE BOARD, AND OBJECTS.

I wish most emphatically to state that any branch of drawing in any of the grades of schools, which cannot be taught to all alike in a class by class instruction given by the regular teacher, helped by such diagrams and illustrations as the teacher makes for or before the pupils, and strengthened, if need be, by repetition of examples used as materials in instruction, as, for instance, natural objects, casts, etc.; in other words, any exercises involved by teaching drawing which necessitate the individual instruction of pupils ought not to find a place in the common-school class-room.

Correction of the work of individuals is as necessary in drawing as in language or arithmetic; but it should be the correction of individual errors made in working from class instruction, and this only to supplement the teaching of general principles, which the pupil has misunderstood, or has not attended to the explanation of. For the teacher to do more than this for individuals is eminently unjust to all concerned. No teacher with between thirty and fifty pupils to instruct in a short time can give private lessons on separate works to all, and that is what the old way of teaching with flat copies, each a different subject, really involved; but there is ample time to give full and complete explanation and instruction to a class of any size within eyesight of an object or the blackboard, and within earshot of the teacher, if the teaching be given by class instruction from one subject or object for all the pupils at the same time. And the exercises of individuals must be treated in this subject as in any other, — viz., be examined and corrected, if need be, by the standard of the principles taught; and that should be the form and limit of the individual teaching given to each pupil.

This limitation also proscribes all fanciful freaks, likes, and dislikes of individuals as to subject, and excludes from the course of study all objectionable branches and subjects which involve loss of time for both teacher and pupil, and which, being in the nature of amusement or recreation, convey nothing of general interest and consequence, or of educational value.

Such a change as is indicated by this mode of class instruction would be necessitated by the discontinuance of special instructors in the high schools, even if it were not the best method under any circumstances, as I claim it to be for the common schools of all grades.

Under the departmental plan of teaching in schools, all the teachers are special teachers, with the exception of the principal; and where that is the case the drawing-teacher, as a specialist, is in his right place: but even then the class system, by one general lesson to all, as distinguished from the present method of teaching each pupil on a separate copy, is infinitely preferable to the latter.

If it should be found that good results do not immediately follow such a plan, it will yet be something to have discountenanced the wrong principle of giving private lessons in public schools, and to have established the right method of instruction in drawing as a part of the common-school system.

Should satisfactory results not immediately appear, the explanation will be found in one of the three following reasons: viz., —

1. The subject of instruction is not suitable to the common schools, or a legitimate part of general education ; or,

2. The scheme is not well arranged and graduated, and the pupils are therefore not well prepared in the lower classes for what has to be done in the higher; or,

3. The teachers are not competent to give the instruction.

The first and second reasons will not apply to that which you have to teach, or to the plan of instruction which does prepare the grammar-school pupils for high-school work, as evidence obtained during my long experience in the annual or semi-annual examinations conclusively proves. The third cause of failure is remediable where it exists, just as it has already been remedied in the primary and grammar schools. The educational instincts of a good teacher will carry him safely through and over the manual practice required, and he has already learned the more difficult art of simplifying and imparting knowledge to pupils by explanation and demonstration. The best results hitherto obtained from teaching drawing in the high schools have been in the classes wholly taught by the regular teachers,

— not from those which have received instruction from special instructors, whose influence with pupils has been less efficient, and whose normal training less complete. This has been made manifest more and more as the years have passed, and we must accept it as demonstrating a principle which has not yet been sufficiently recognized. It is well for us as citizens that in this matter the interests of education and economy are identical; and a careful observation of work and results for eight years in all the grades of schools convinces me that this is the case. In determining to remove specialists from the high schools, the Committee on Revision meant only to be economical : but they have, without knowing it, advanced a true principle of education ; and the only matter of regret is, that they should not be consistent and apply the rule to all subjects as well as to drawing, though it is a great testimony to the success of drawing that it should be first able to bear the application of so good a rule.

MODEL AND OBJECT DRAWING IN LIGHT AND SHADE.

How this is to be taught by class instruction I shall endeavor to show you by the method I employ in teaching you here. Much of it will consist of applying the laws of linear perspective to drawing from the solid, and the rest to the expression of roundness and distance, realism and intensity, as affected by aërial perspective. You know that it is not convenient nor judicious to teach light and shade in the lower classes before the pupils enter the high schools, though they are taught to draw from objects in outline and true perspective. This new feature of light and shade is therefore but the addition of one more characteristic to the drawing previously practised. I have been accustomed to define the three branches of drawing as (1) Outline, or form ; (2) Outline, and light and shade, or form and roundness ; (3) Outline, light and shade and color, or form, roundness, and tint ; and to describe these degrees of truth in the expression of what we see as being respectively (1) one-third, (2) two-thirds, (3) three-thirds, of the truth. It is not asserted that they are of equal importance in expressing the truth when a drawing has to be made ; but they are distinct features of an object, each susceptible of being truthfully or untruthfully rendered, and the aggregation of these elements determines the value of the drawing as a record.

The same object displayed before a whole class will be seen differently by every member of it (with the single exception of the sphere). How, then, can all be made to draw the object with reasonable accuracy? I would answer this by saying, that, if the class be taught to draw what they see, if clear and radical explanations be given of the possible ways in which the solid or object may be seen, and also in which it cannot be seen, under given conditions, and these explanations be generously full in detail, and exhaustively illustrated by diagrammatic sketches on the board or on paper, as a preceding exercise to the class-work, and accompanying the progress of the pupils, then you may be sure you will open the eyes and educate the perceptive and executive powers of your classes at the same time. The reproduction of these diagrammatic sketches by all the pupils before a subject is commenced will never do harm ; but, if they have been previously well taught, it will not be necessary.

The three materials used most commonly in drawing to obtain effects of light and shade as seen on objects are the pencil or crayon, the stump or leather with carbon, and the brush and one pigment ; the two first being called the dry point, and the last the wet point.

The mode of work peculiar to each, and the effects obtainable, you will see illustrated by your own practice here ; and it is not to be denied that the mastery over these tools and implements will be something of a struggle to you at your age, but the young people will not be troubled by it. It will be necessary for you to do the very worst you can, and make every mistake possible, whilst under my tuition, in order that I may show you the cause of your failure and the way out of it ; for that is what you will have to do for your own pupils next year. You need not fear that I shall be displeased or discouraged by your efforts if they are not masterpieces. By no means ! The only discouragement to a good teacher is when his pupils telescope their faculties, and do nothing, waiting for something to be done for them ; and then that is a hopeless business, meaning nothing all round, nothing for you to learn, nothing for me to teach, — blank generally.

I hope we are too old to commit educational suicide in that way ; and so I shall expect you all to do the best, as well as the worst you can, with all the light you have, and thus give me the opportunity to show you how to make it the best possible by correcting your mistakes whilst they are yet young.

It is a golden rule in teaching that you cannot teach that which you do not know, and, except in singing (when your own voice has gone, though you once were able), you cannot make a pupil do that which you are unable to do yourself. So the only way to make a clean sweep of your pupils' difficulties is to feel and destroy those same troubles in your own experience; and then you will feel at home and happy in your class-rooms when the youthful artists begin to experience the inevitable troubles incidental to early practice with point or stump or brush, and to make all the mistakes possible to the callow powers of a fallen race.

If you will be faithful to me, and show me all that you do not know and cannot do, when called upon to record your knowledge on a typical exercise, I will be faithful to you, and show you what I do know and what is known on the same thing.

And, fellow-teachers, let us try to realize that the best work of art is only an approximation to the truth, not a realization of it; so that, in our own works, and more especially in those of our pupils, we must only expect a modest approach to the expression of true drawing. even when we and they have done our best. I have very seldom seen a painting or a drawing, either by old or modern masters, so called, that has not displayed some childish error in the simple matter of perspective, and most of them are crowded with diabolical mistakes in drawing. The artists who have been graphic scholars, who have spoken grammatically truly, as the sun speaks and as science interprets, are to be counted on the fingers of one hand without exhausting the fingers.

Study form as you would mathematics, study beauty as you do Greek and Latin verse, study expression as you do study it in music, and study truth as you would in a chemical analysis, and then apply this test to the productions of all artists, — including those who have picked up a vagrant education by rule of thumb, or depend on what they consider the inspiration of genius, — and you will find that the world has produced but two art scholars, Phidias and Michael Angelo. The rest have been generally wandering in the wilderness, seeking vainly after the truth, many of them ignorant even of the language in which she speaks. I go to exhibitions of modern paintings only to find efforts at oratory which are not even decent enough to

be grammatical, and see attempts to embody heroic achieve-
ments rendered by people who are too gifted to tell the truth
about that which they are 'supposed to know; from which one
may draw the inference that their imagination is mere crude
speculation, and their sentiment, bathos. Their habits being
unequal to the demand of the true, they are incapable of rising
to the appreciation and expression of the beautiful.

I bring this before you, high-school teachers, because people
are accustomed to surround the subject of art with a halo and a
glamour of mystery; to shake their heads, and hint at divine
gifts, when men of intelligence and brains venture to look into
the mysteries of expressed art. As a professionally educated
artist and graduate of a national art school, I would say that
there is nothing in modern art and nothing in the subject itself
which a cultured man is unable to understand with very little
study. In fact, tried by the standards of the past, by which
some departments of human intelligence and performance would
not suffer, our modern art work may be fully described as the
apotheosis of insufficiency; so that neither you nor I need feel
very frightened at modestly taking up this matter of teaching
the elements of an art which has been so very imperfectly understood in the past, and is so very imperfectly practised at the
present time.

The cause of this deficiency is the absence in the past of the
systematic education in the elements of art which we are called
upon to give in the public schools; and when this has been given
for a generation or two we shall see, or those who succeed us
will see, a more intelligent and nobler art than has ever been
possible without such foundation work as that we are now at-
tempting.

COLOR.

The practice in color which seems suitable to pupils in high
schools, and which is practicable of attainment in the class-
rooms there, consists of studying the historical ornament of
such styles as employed color in their ornamental art as an introduction to the use of the pigments and brush, and afterwards the study from objects, natural and others, such as may
be easily obtained by teachers and pupils. During one term of
half a year a good subject of any of the great historic styles
may be executed by the class from large diagrams made by the
teacher, and reproduced by him before the class whilst they are

doing the same thing. Three or four lessons of two hours each will be ample time to accomplish such work; and, if the amount to be done at each lesson be shown by a separate diagram, the first giving the outline and the following ones each advancing the work one stage further towards completion, a whole class can thus be instructed together, and learn to accomplish by clear and distinct steps a definite amount of work in a given time, and in the right way. Every teacher should produce such illustrations as are required to make his class understand the subject and the processes, made on a large scale, so that all may see them distinctly, and thus lead up to the drawing and painting from nature and objects, which is to follow the exercises in historic ornament.

In selecting natural objects for the subjects of lessons, fruits which are of one color, — such as the orange, lemon, and others of the same character, — first singly, and then grouped to give contrast in tint, are the best for early practice. And there is a variety of excellent materials for lessons in vegetables, so that with the objects and vases and other forms to be sometimes found in the class-rooms, or which may be brought there, there is ample material with which to give the one or two subject-lessons to each class during the term.

I need not go into further details of the work you will have to do when the responsibility rests wholly upon you for all the instruction in drawing given in the high schools; for the best illustrations I could give you will be in your own practice of that work here and now. The method of instruction, as applied to such exercises as we shall go through, is a new one, though it has developed as a natural growth from our experience in the lower grades of schools. It will no doubt be subjected to criticism both by those who practise other ways of teaching, and by some who know nothing of the subject, as new ways or new adaptations of old ways usually are. In this matter we are all pioneers, and have to be subject to the strain and the toil of travelling over new ground or on disputed territory with all the pains and penalties implied. But I have no doubt of the success which will attend your efforts, nor of the benefit to education involved by that success.

Finally, fellow-teachers of the high schools, I place myself unreservedly at your service the first three days of the school week, being advised by the Drawing Committee that this is especially the work of the year. I am obliged to say for the first three days only, because the last days of my week belong to the State. If, therefore, there is any way that occurs to any of you by which my knowledge of this subject can be brought to bear, so as to assist you in the work you have to do, please make the suggestion freely and fully, either by letter or at an interview; and, after consultation with the chairman of the Drawing Committee, I will endeavor to comply with your wishes. My own reputation professionally is at stake in this matter. I was called to my position here in city and State to organize a plan of instruction, and see it carried out in the schools. The progress made in the lower grades of schools now makes it possible to put the higher grades and evening schools into their proper places in the educational chain. It never has been possible before, because the pupils have not until now been prepared to take the more advanced instruction. But I think that, if you will allow me to co-operate with you, we shall be able next year to begin the crowning of the fabric, and thus carry out the decisions of the School Committee with reference to the high schools. I have perfect faith in the wisdom and the practicability of the proposal, and those of you who do not at present share with me in this faith will grow into it. And, as perpetual growth is the sign of the living teacher, I take the liberty to hope that we may all live forever.